DATE DUE

FUN FACT FILE: FIERCE FISH!

20 FUN FACTS ABOUT ANGLERFISH

By Heather Moore Niver

Gareth Stevens Publishing

Please visit our website, www.garethstevens.com. For a free color catalog of all our high-quality books, call toll free 1-800-542-2595 or fax 1-877-542-2596.

Library of Congress Cataloging-in-Publication Data

Niver, Heather Moore.
20 fun facts about anglerfish / Heather Moore Niver.
p. cm. — (Fun fact file: fierce fish!)
Includes index.
ISBN 978-1-4339-6972-0 (pbk.)
ISBN 978-1-4339-6973-7 (6-pack)
ISBN 978-1-4339-6971-3 (library binding)
1. Anglerfishes—Juvenile literature. I. Title. II. Title: Twenty fun facts about anglerfish.
QL637.9.L6N58 2012
597'.62—dc23

2011047707

First Edition

Published in 2013 by
Gareth Stevens Publishing
111 East 14th Street, Suite 349
New York, NY 10003

Designer: Ben Gardner
Editor: Greg Roza

Photo credits: Cover Darlyne A. Murawwski/National Geographic/Getty Images; cover, pp. 1, 7, 22, 26, 29 Shutterstock.com; pp. 5, 8 Jeff Rotman/The Image Bank/Getty Images; p. 6 David B. Fleetham/Oxford Scientific/Getty Images; p. 9 Jeffery L. Rotman/Peter Arnold/Getty Images; p. 10 Daniela Dirscherl/Waterframe/Getty Images; p. 11 Secret Sea Visions/Peter Arnold/Getty Images; p. 12 Dante Fenolio/Photo Researchers/Getty Images; p. 13 Jason Isle-Scubazoo/Science Faction/Getty Images; p. 14 Fredrik Ehrenstrom/Oxford Scientific/Getty Images; pp. 15, 17, 18 Peter David/Taxi/Getty Images; p. 16 Doug Perrine/Peter Arnold/Getty Images; p. 20–21 Visual Unlimited, Inc. Reinhard Dirscheri/Visuals Unlimited/Getty Images; p. 23 Neil Bromhall/Oxford Scientific/Getty Images; p. 24 Clive Bromhall/Oxford Scientific/Getty Images; p. 25 Jonathan Bird/Peter Arnold/Getty Images; p. 27 David Doubilet/Contributor/National Geographic/Getty Images.

Printed in the United States of America

CPSIA compliance information: Batch #CS12GS: For further information contact Gareth Stevens, New York, New York at 1-800-542-2595.

Contents

Words in the glossary appear in **bold** type the first time they are used in the text.

Creepy Creatures

Way down deep in the ocean, it's cold and dark. Sunlight doesn't reach that deep. But this part of the ocean isn't lacking in life. Some critters make their home along the ocean floor. Anglerfish might be the most unusual fish living in the deep sea.

Anglerfish look like something from outer space! They may not be known for their good looks, but they're funky fish. So dive into the world of anglerfish and learn more about these deep-sea swimmers.

This anglerfish is also known as a hairy frogfish.

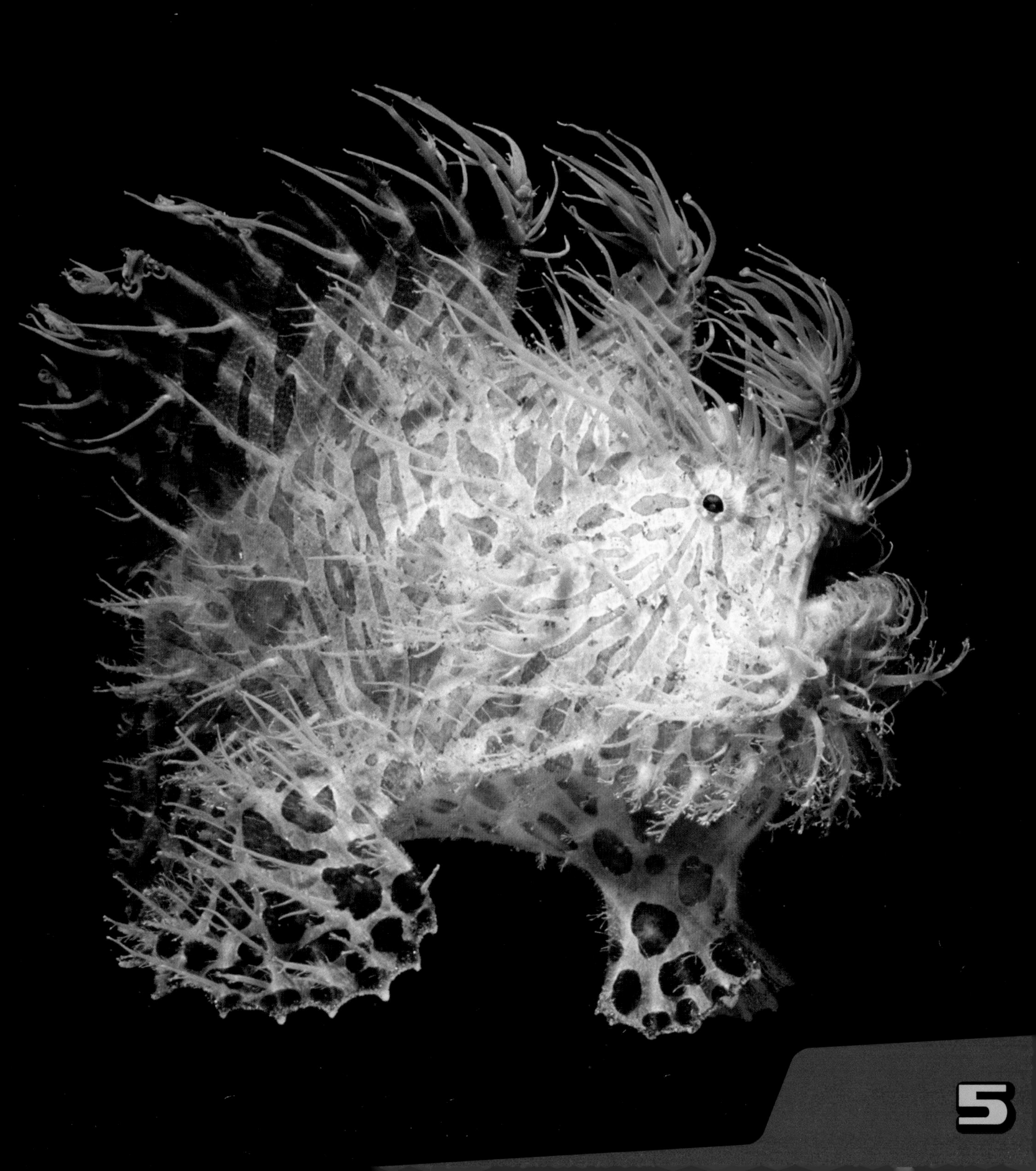

Spotting an Anglerfish

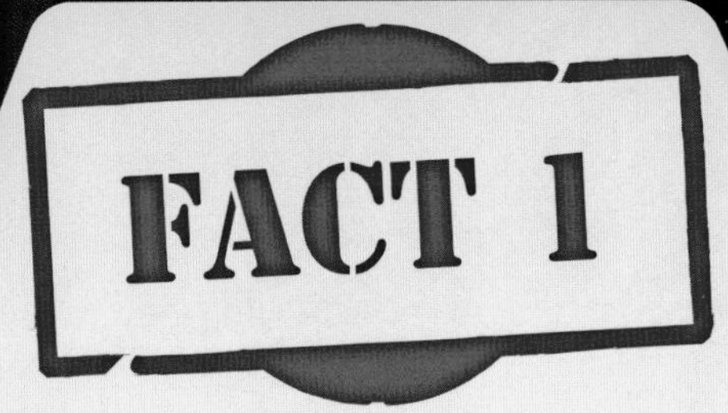

Close to 300 kinds of anglerfish are swimming in Earth's seas.

There are nearly 300 species, or kinds, of anglerfish. They include goosefish, batfish, deep-sea anglerfish, and common anglerfish. The common anglerfish is also called the frogfish. Another name for the deep-sea anglerfish is "common black devil."

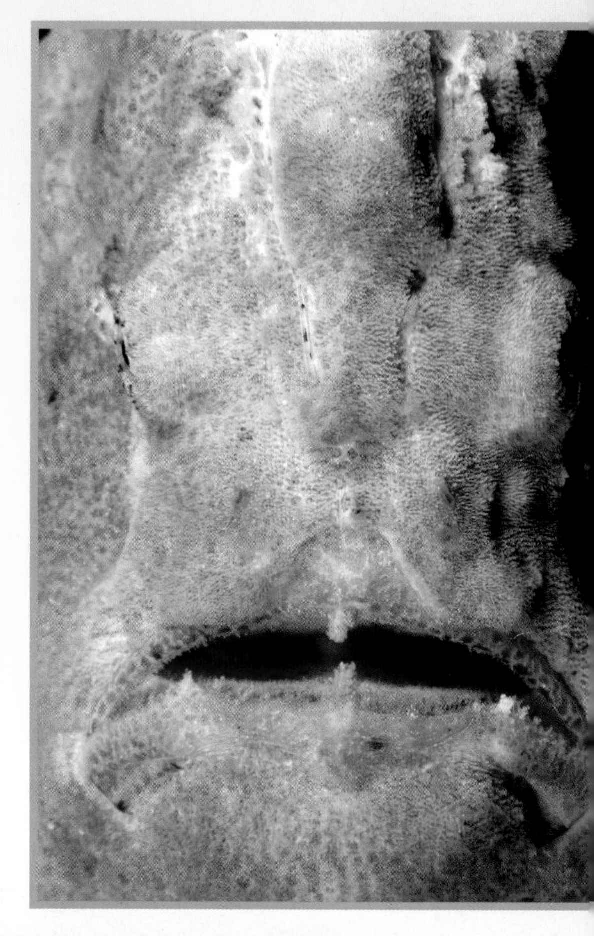

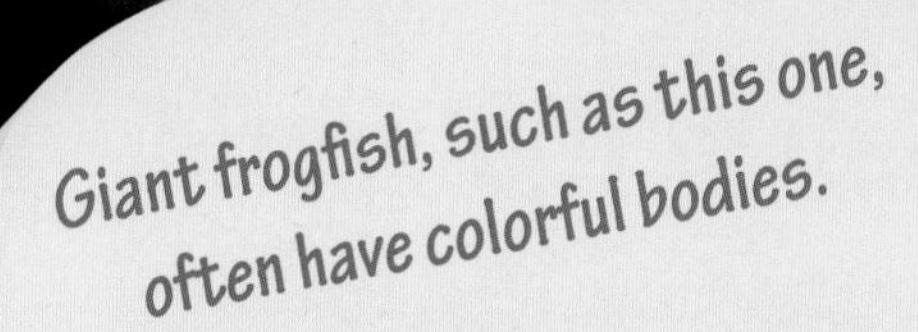
Giant frogfish, such as this one, often have colorful bodies.

FACT 2

Anglerfish can live 1 mile (1.6 km) below the ocean's surface.

Most anglerfish live in the Atlantic and the Antarctic Oceans. Their **habitat** is usually on the seafloor a mile deep, but some live in more shallow **tropical** waters. Frogfish also live in shallow water off the coast of Europe.

Finned Fashion

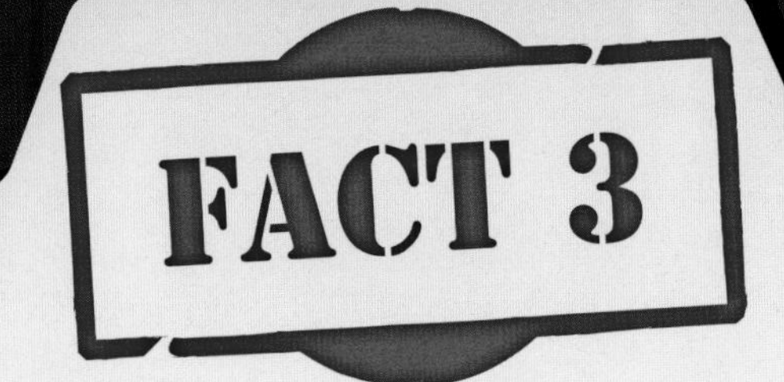

In 2006, scientists named the male of one anglerfish species the smallest fish in the world.

Female anglerfish are usually between 8 inches (20.3 cm) and 3.3 feet (1 m) long. Males are much smaller than females. The smallest male anglerfish are only about a quarter of an inch (6.4 mm) long.

Many frogfish are colorful, but most anglerfish are dark colors such as gray or brown.

Anglerfish skin sometimes has specks or other patterns.

FACT 4

Deep-sea anglerfish fall apart when touched.

Instead of scales like most fish have, deep-sea anglerfish have thin skin. It's so thin that it slips right off if a person tries to pick up the fish. Anglerfish have weak, floppy **muscles**. Their bones aren't very strong, either.

Dinnertime!

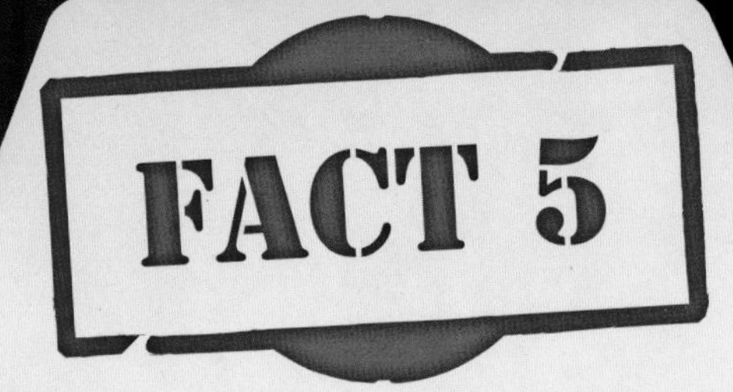

Frogfish can change colors.

Anglerfish like to blend with their surroundings. Some frogfish can change color to look more like coral or the ocean floor. Most have bumpy skin that looks like their surroundings. This helps them hide and wait for **prey**.

Frogfish may change color in a few seconds, or the change might take weeks.

An anglerfish can swallow food more than twice its own size.

Anglerfish like to eat small fish. Sometimes they enjoy a nice meal of shrimp or crabs. Anglerfish have such big mouths and bendable bodies that they can swallow prey more than twice their own size!

Check out the big mouth on this frogfish!

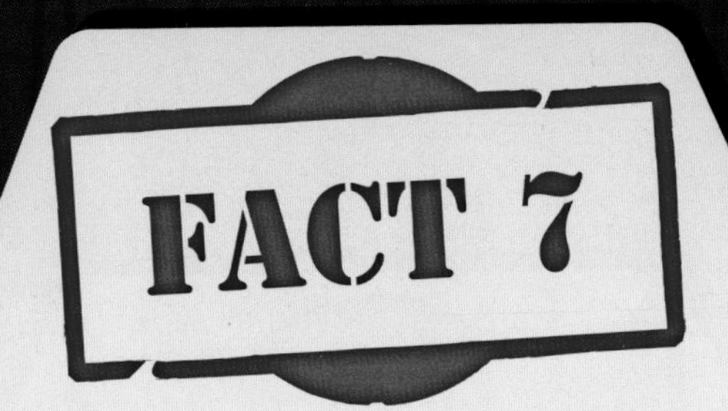

Some anglerfish have teeth that fold back so their food can slide right past.

An anglerfish's teeth look really scary! Some anglerfish have hooked teeth to help trap prey. Deep-sea anglerfish have huge mouths filled with pointy, **translucent** teeth. Their teeth even fold backward to make more room for food.

Frogfish also chow down on seabirds.

FACT 8

Frogfish suck in their food and swallow it in less time than it takes for you to blink.

Unlike their deep-sea cousins, frogfish don't have any teeth. Instead, the frogfish sucks its food in and swallows it whole. It does this in less than 1/100 of a second—faster than any other fish! Juices in its stomach take care of breaking down the food.

FACT 9

Deep-sea anglerfish will eat almost anything that swims past.

Anglerfish that live in the deep sea don't have many dinner choices. Few tasty fish live in those dark waters. Anglerfish rarely allow a fish to swim by without trying to eat it. They never know when their next meal will swim by.

Gone Fishing

The anglerfish has its own "fishing pole."

The female anglerfish has a special **spine** called a fin ray. It sticks out over the front of her head like a fishing pole. Anglerfish use this fin ray to **lure** prey closer to them so it's easier to catch.

An "angler" is a person who fishes with a fishing pole. This is how the anglerfish got its name.

Glow-in-the-Dark Fish

Some anglerfish can make their own light.

It's very dark at the bottom of the ocean. However, some anglerfish make their own light! They have special **bacteria** in a bulb at the end of their fin ray. The bacteria shines and helps them see prey.

This anglerfish was found 3,300 feet (1,000 m) below the water's surface near Hawaii.

The lure on many anglerfish grows out of their heads. However, some are located on the back or even in the mouth.

FACT 12

Anglerfish can turn their light on whenever they want.

When anglerfish sense prey nearby, they turn on their light. The prey swims toward it. Little does it know that the anglerfish is just waiting for a tasty meal. When the fish swims close enough—CHOMP! It's dinnertime for the anglerfish.

FACT 13

Some anglerfish can make their light flash.

Just having a light in the dark water doesn't mean the anglerfish will get its meal. Prey may sense danger and swim away. Some anglerfish can make their bright bulb spin and flash. This lures their prey close enough to be eaten.

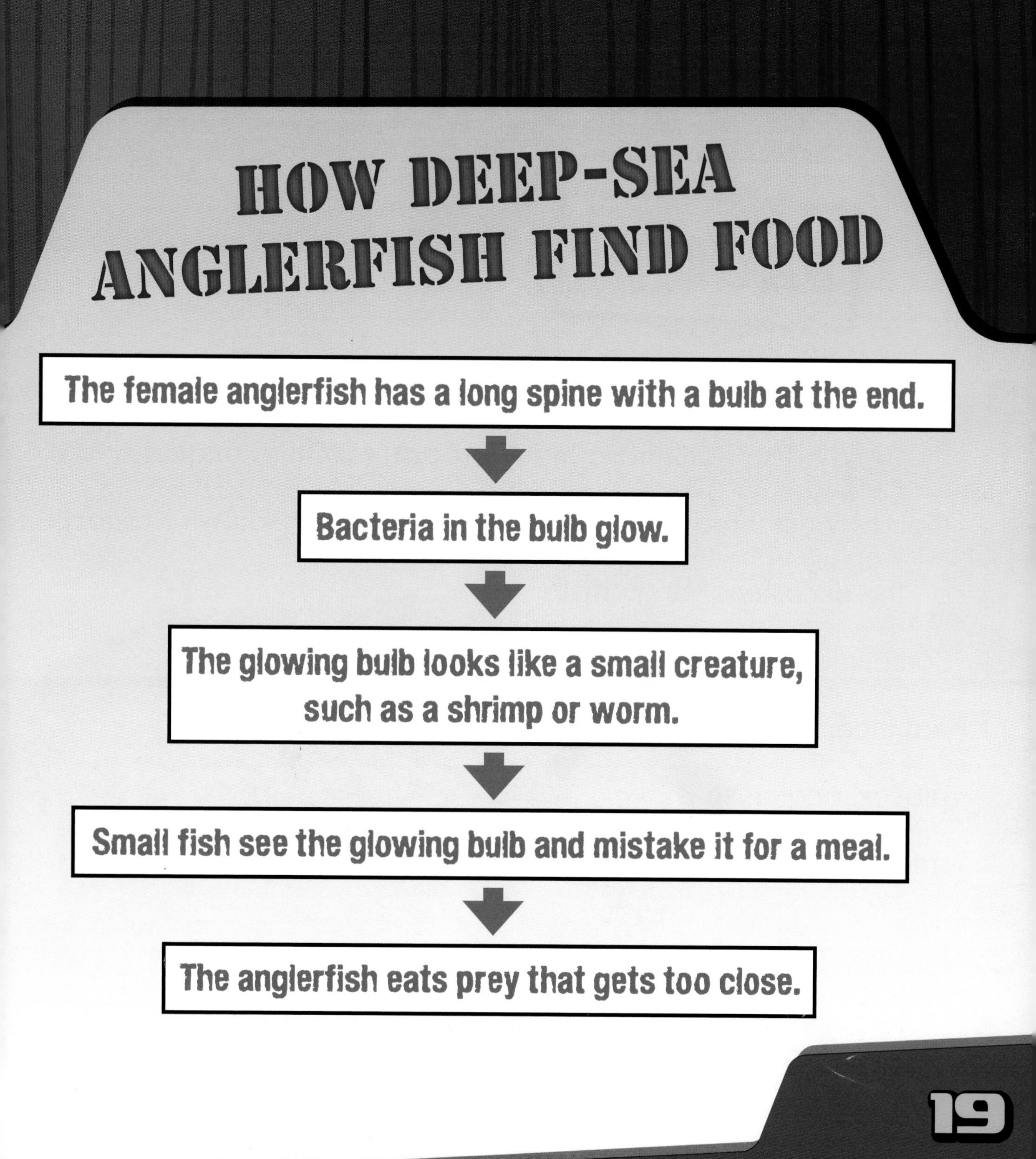

HOW DEEP-SEA ANGLERFISH FIND FOOD

The female anglerfish has a long spine with a bulb at the end.

↓

Bacteria in the bulb glow.

↓

The glowing bulb looks like a small creature, such as a shrimp or worm.

↓

Small fish see the glowing bulb and mistake it for a meal.

↓

The anglerfish eats prey that gets too close.

FACT 14

Anglerfish don't have many other fish to fear.

Anglerfish don't have many **predators**. Other anglerfish are their biggest threat. Moray eels have also been known to snack on the occasional anglerfish. Sometimes people eat them, too. In some places, anglerfish is a fancy treat.

These Fins Were Made for . . . Walking?

FACT 15

Female anglerfish aren't good swimmers.

Most female anglerfish, like the deep-sea anglerfish, have a ball-shaped body. This body shape isn't great for quick bursts of swimming. But the anglerfish can float in place for long periods of time as it waits for prey to swim by.

The short-spined anglerfish has a body that looks like the rocks where it lives. This allows it to hide easily.

This frogfish is also called a clown anglerfish.

FACT 16

Frogfish use their fins to "walk" around.

Frogfish use their fins somewhat like frogs use their legs. Their fins help them move along the ocean floor or through coral reefs to hide and wait for their next meal. Frogfish are also short and round, like the animals they're named after.

Oh Baby!

FACT 17

Male anglerfish are better swimmers than females.

Male anglerfish don't have a very exciting life. Shortly after a male is born, he starts looking for a female. Males have stronger muscles than females. This allows them to swim long distances in search of a **mate**.

male

emale

Some scientists think that the female anglerfish gives off a smell that draws males to her.

A male anglerfish stays joined to a female for the rest of his life.

Once a male anglerfish finds a female, he bites her and holds on. Soon after, the male and female fuse, which means their tissues grow together. The female gives the male food and oxygen. The male **fertilizes** the female's eggs so they can have babies.

Up to six males may fuse with a single female over the course of her life.

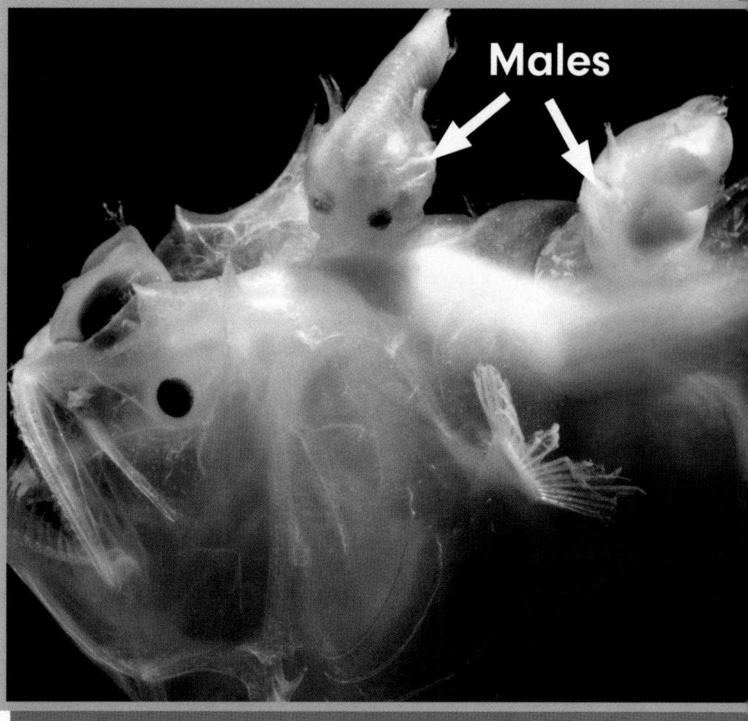

FACT 19

A female frogfish can lay up to 180,000 eggs.

As an anglerfish mom fills up with eggs, she stretches out and begins to float. The male helps move her to the surface. The female lays the eggs in a thin, jelly-like raft. Young anglerfish eat **plankton** until they're old enough to swim deeper.

FACT 20

Scientists aren't totally sure how long anglerfish live.

Anglerfish probably only live about 3 years. Most fish studies occur in **fisheries**, but anglerfish don't usually live there. In **captivity**, anglerfish only live a few years, so scientists think they probably have even shorter lives in the wild.

ANGLERFISH FRIENDS

common name	number of species	length
batfish	68	10 inches (25 cm)
goosefish (monkfish)	25	3.3 feet (1 m)
frogfish (common anglerfish)	43	14 inches (36 cm)
deep-sea anglerfish (common black devil)	160	3.9 feet (1.2 m)

Awesome Anglerfish

Anglerfish live in such deep, dark waters that it's not easy to get pictures and information about them. Sometimes the fish blend in with their surroundings so well that divers don't even see them. Scientists have to be creative to learn about these creepy creatures.

There are some pretty neat creatures living down in the freezing cold waters of the deep sea. Maybe their way of life seems strange, but it's pretty interesting to learn about what goes on 1 mile (1.6 km) beneath the water's surface.

The clown anglerfish is one of the more colorful anglerfish in the sea.

bacteria: tiny creatures that can only be seen with a microscope

captivity: the state of being caged

fertilize: to cause an egg to grow into a new animal

fishery: a place where fish are raised

habitat: an area where plants, animals, and other living things live

lure: to draw an animal closer in order to catch it. Also, an object used to bring an animal closer.

mate: one of two animals that come together to make a baby

muscle: one of the parts of the body that allow movement

plankton: a tiny plant or animal that floats in the ocean

predator: an animal that hunts other animals for food

prey: an animal hunted by other animals for food

spine: a long, pointy part on an animal

translucent: allowing light to pass through

tropical: having to do with the warm parts of Earth near the equator

For More Information

Books

Coldiron, Deborah. *Anglerfish*. Edina, MN: ABDO Publishing Company, 2008.

Lynette, Rachel. *Deep-Sea Anglerfish and Other Fearsome Fish*. Chicago, IL: Raintree, 2012.

Pipe, Jim. *Scary Creatures of the Deep*. New York, NY: Franklin Watts, 2009.

Websites

Anglerfish
animals.nationalgeographic.com/animals/fish/anglerfish/
Learn more about anglerfish with facts, photos, and maps.

Anglerfish
www.arkive.org/anglerfish/lophius-piscatorius/#text=All
Watch anglerfish videos, see pictures, and read more facts.

Deep Sea Anglerfish
www.seasky.org/deep-sea/anglerfish.html
Check out great photos and facts about the deep-sea anglerfish and other underwater creatures.

Index